EMPLOYMENT ESSENTIALS™

COLLEGE EDITION

ISBN: 1463519621
ISBN 13: 9781463519629
Library of Congress Control Number: 2011908718
CreateSpace, North Charleston, South Carolina

This book is dedicated to my children, without whose support and love would have made this project simply instructional, and not a work from the heart.

"I feel like just another,
Spoke in a great big wheel,
Like a tiny blade of grass
in a great big field."

Bob Seger, "Feel Like A Number"

"By failing to prepare, you are preparing to fail."

Benjamin Franklin

Contents

Introduction

My motivation for sharing *Employment Essentials* happened as a result of many years of witnessing my own children, plus many other young and highly energetic applicants, come to the interview process without any knowledge of the methods involved in selling themselves. All were after the same result, a good position with a stable company, but few had the background information necessary to make the interview into what it really is:

• An opportunity for the interviewer to collect facts

• An opportunity for the applicant to reveal his or her capabilities

Today, with social networking growing exponentially, it has almost worsened the situation for new applicants. Posting résumés and cover letters to an undefined place in space that has no interest in you or what you bring to the table evokes a general feeling of accomplishment once completed. The truth, particularly for the new college graduate with a limited job history to exploit, is that posting your résumé is just one of many steps included in the successful job search. Additionally, posting your résumé before you have done the requisite work to prepare could lead to a disappointing start to your career. Social networking is taking the world to new levels of sharing and communication, and I will not understate its role in job awareness, but before you can work effectively to find opportunities through the many social networks available today, you must do the required work to prepare. Once prepared for all steps of gaining employment, the social networks enhance your ability to find a job that you desire.

Employment Essentials helps people gain employment by enabling them to outperform other applicants during the rigorous process of securing a job and then a career.

About This Process

This process, and the roadmap it provides, is not simply a compilation of ideas and tips meant to give advice on specific job topics. That can be found in any number of sources, and they generally do not offer much help in gaining individual employment.

What follows is a self-empowering process that has proven effective for those I have counseled. I did not give them abbreviated direction, nor will I give it to you. This process depends on interaction, and it begins with defining your product, the most important product you will ever promote: you.

If you allow your mind to embrace new ideas, spend personal time defining that which you desire most, and then follow the roadmap, I know through experience that you will leap ahead of others competing for the same opportunity. The information contained in this document comes from real-life experience and is an in-depth, dynamic tool that will empower you to create a winning job outcome.

Step 1
Getting Started

First of all, take a deep breath and relax. We are going to focus on you for the next several hours. It is an investment that pays you directly and much sooner than you think. I know the pressures of gaining that first job, being out of work, and/or being short on cash, but you are not out of time. You can take control of this opportunity by dedicating yourself completely to gaining employment. Common thought dictates that you should work at this task as hard as you will work upon receiving employment, so your job today is to get prepared. The time you spend in preparation actually decreases the overall time it takes to attain your goal. Companies always need good employees, regardless of the economy, and this overview will help you:

- Highlight your skills
- Showcase your desire, enabling you to rise above other applicants

For this exercise, I used an applicant with a Bachelor of Science degree in chemistry. For those of you graduating in other fields outside of chemistry, such as accounting, business, history, teaching, pharmacy and so forth you can replace the chemistry piece with your own specialty.

Defining Your Goal

Before you start randomly posting résumés to social networks, companies, or recruiters, you should do the following:

1. Make a list of the job categories (the functions you want to perform in the companies you choose) you are willing to pursue. For example, the chemist could select bench chemistry in Quantitative Analysis or Organic Chemistry. For an accounting graduate, it could be general accounting, cost accounting, or payroll. Marketing could include market analyst, product management, marketing communication, and so forth. Just define for yourself the area in which you most want to work, but remember, the goal is to gain employment first, so you may have to take a different position to get started.

2. Spend a few hours looking at different job qualifications on the Internet. In the next point, I suggest an easy method for finding information on the job category you wish to enter.

3. Stack-rank them in order of preference weighted against your qualifications. Stack-ranking is simply aligning your preferences in numerical order, with the most desirable position labeled as 1, the second as 2, and so forth. It is as simple as typing "entry-level jobs" into your browser with your background qualifications (e.g., "entry-level job and chemistry") and your city or state.

If you put in the sweat equity needed in Step 1, the results for the following steps become easier to attain. You are on the right path, so stop for a few minutes, relax, and feel the self-empowerment developing within you. You are already becoming a winner in the race for employment.

Example

You have (or will soon have) graduated with a Bachelor of Science degree in chemistry from a state university. Here are a few examples of industries demanding your expertise:[1]

- Chemicals
- Pharmaceuticals
- Hospitals
- Federal/state agencies performing chemical testing
- Industrial chemistry
- Food and beverage
- Environmental
- Personal care
- Veterinary chemistry
- Physician offices
- Department of Defense
- Homeland Security
- Military
- And many more.

---

1 The number of positions in your area of interest can be easily found through the U.S. Bureau of Labor Statistics or any number of sites that will come up under your search.

Level 1 refers to an entry level position. Oftentimes, especially in the scientific field, positions are assigned levels indicating experience and proficiency of company standards for that particular job function. It follows, then, that once you are proficient in a Level 1 position, Level 2 would be a logical step. In general business positions, the terminology is a bit different. A Level 1 position may be labeled assistant, then associate, and so forth.

These specific companies need chemists for general chemistry testing on products, specimens, research projects, and so forth. All products must pass rigorous quality control standards, and the chemist at the bench often tests for acceptable quality. Incoming materials used to manufacture products must also be tested.

Once you have searched, you can stack-rank the top ten positions that capture your interest. Ten is an arbitrary number I selected as it keeps your job search focused and easy to manage. I would suggest that you keep a considerable number of possible jobs in your pipeline so that when one of the first ten drops out, you have an immediate ability to replace it with a new opportunity. See Attachment 1, Stack-Ranking Your Employment Search.

Is Your Goal Realistic?

Realism is important here, and it requires you to be truthful with yourself. Do not be daunted if you take a lesser position than what you desired as a first step, as that will allow you to get into the company of choice and then progress with time. Study the qualifications listed for positions, and then ask yourself if:

- You qualify for this position today, or

- You could grow into this position by first gaining experience in the organization.

I have several personal stories I could tell, but let me relate one to give an example of how this can work.

Example

I counseled a young lady who had recently earned her Bachelor of Science degree in Pharmaceutical Sciences. She knew she wanted to work in clinical studies. She had the background to add value in clinical studies, but the requirements for clinical study work usually require a Master of Science degree. She wisely signed on with a company to work in their sterile laboratory as a first step. She is gaining experience, and, as she becomes known at her current company, the chances of gaining the clinical study position will become much better with time. Most companies prefer employees with training in their methods of operation, and she will be given an opportunity for more demanding work in the future due to her enthusiasm and perseverance.

Note

Keep this in your notes for use in Step 5. When interviewing for a position, the interviewer may state that your qualifications are excellent, but the position of interest requires more education or experience. Many untrained candidates simply say, "Thank you for your time" and leave feeling rejected. You can turn this apparent rejection into an opportunity. Simply acknowledge that you understand the situation. Then follow up by asking if other positions for which you are better qualified are open. Say you would be more than interested in exploring those. Try this, for example, "Thank you for the information, it helps me understand the situation. Is there another opportunity within your company where my background could be utilized? I would certainly be willing to look at other opportunities." It is difficult for anyone in a hiring position to turn down enthusiasm. You will never win a job if you don't ask. Go for it. You have nothing to lose, and you will, at minimum, walk away knowing you gave it your best.

Review Step 1 of 8
What have you discovered thus far?

1. **Define your goal.** The time you spend in studying job categories with your particular skill sets will help shorten the time to employment immensely. Knowledge is power. You certainly don't complete the process by spending an hour on the Internet. It requires several hours daily in researching the myriad of companies that utilize your skill sets. Many more companies than what you could ever imagine require your background. Don't be afraid to look for these hidden gems. Let me give an example. Most chemistry graduates think of laboratories in pure chemical analysis, such as medicine, pharmaceuticals, and industrial chemical manufacturers. While this is true, don't overlook food, beverage, cosmetic, paints and coatings, and so on. The list is endless, which improves your odds immensely.

2. **Stack-rank your favorite picks of future jobs.** Don't be afraid of an industry that you are unfamiliar with. If it sounds exciting, it might be the right pick for you.

3. **Be realistic and honest with yourself.** You have a whole career to climb the career mountain. Take one level at a time.

Congratulations! You are ready to move on to the next step in your journey.

Step 2
Beginning the Search

How Do You Start?

We have already discussed stack-ranking your job preferences. Now the real fun begins. Once you decide that you want to become a chemist in the industrial foods market, or other market of your choice, you now have several factors to consider.

This list could become exhausting, but the following captures most of what you need to focus on first:

- Do you want to stay local to your present location?

- If locality is secondary to the job, where are you willing to relocate geographically?

- Does the geography support several companies that utilize your skill set?

- Will you be able to locate by friends or family if that is important to you?

- Can you afford to live in the area adjacent to the workplace, or would you have long commutes for more affordable living areas?[2]

---

2 You can easily check salary ranges for your job category in the *Occupational Outlook Handbook* published by the U.S. Bureau of Labor Statistics.

- Are you willing to work odd shift hours to attain a position?

- Does the area support your lifestyle?

Once you have answered the above questions, you are ready to start—and you always start with yourself.

Building a Selling Résumé, Regardless of Experience

Now it is time to build your résumé. Many résumé-building programs and services are available to you on the Internet, in bookstores, and even advertised on TV. These résumé professionals are excellent at what they do, but I only advise you spend the money for an entry-level position if you have the extra money to spend. I honestly recommend you use public domain templates. These informative templates are available on the Internet to anyone at no charge under various offerings that are unrestricted for use. For your purpose, résumé and cover letters are readily available. Many templates are furnished in the software you may be using today. The formatting of the résumé is important, but the content is really more vital to your search.

Of course, as all courses emphasize, you must capture attention with the résumé and cover letter, so let's begin with the résumé. You can find a résumé format in Attachment 2. Now, let's talk about content, and you, my friend, are the product! The following steps provide you with a start. On your résumé:

1. Define what you want in a job.

2. Briefly describe your qualifications.

3. Match those qualifications to the needs of your target company.

Example Résumé Header: Personalized to the Company (Preferred)

OBJECTIVES

An analytical chemist position utilizing my education, enthusiasm, and laboratory expertise to help drive superior testing results for the quantitative chemistry analysis position posted for Spectacular Chemistry Company.

This example is clean and right to the point. More important, you have personalized the résumé according to the needs of the company where you are applying. You don't have to say any more in the requirement statement than what you are looking for in a prospective company.

Example: Generic to a Social Networking Group, Recruiter, or Cold Call (Acceptable)

OBJECTIVES

A bench chemistry position utilizing my education, enthusiasm, and laboratory expertise to help drive superior testing results in a company requiring advanced chemistry analysis within the laboratory department.

This example is clean as well and right to the point, but opens up a more generalized search that you will probably utilize in parallel with your personal searches. As you will see, I highly recommend using the research and development approach found in the next step, but sending a generic copy to companies you do not have time to research will add to your exposure. The old saying "Even a blind chicken occasionally finds a kernel of corn" applies.

Some experts disagree on formatting. One camp says you have to make the first statements stand out and urge bolding and underlining as quick methods to highlight your abilities. Others say the statement itself is enough. As one who has perused many résumés, I recommend using the first approach as it catches the attention of the reader and I believe creates a higher likelihood of putting that résumé in the callback file.

Now let's discuss your professional experience. What did you say? You don't have any professional experience? I beg to differ. Let me explain.

Do you feel like this dude about professional experience?

First-time entrants often get butterflies. They do not feel they have much experience at all, let alone any professional EXPERIENCE, but THIS isn't true in most cases. Let's go back to the graduate we discussed earlier in this guide, the college chemist intent on a bench chemistry position who needs to begin making money while he finds a career. After all, unless you are personally wealthy, we all work for money and personal satisfaction... and, of course, cars and apartments commensurate to our attitudes.

Professional/Educational Experience

It is time to look in the proverbial mirror once more and define those truthful facts about your background. Let's see:

- You did some lab assisting in college.

- You did win the Crystal Beaker award...even though your roommate used it as a beer stein and shattered it after a few too many at the graduation party.

- During all of your summer breaks from college, you worked at Pills-4-U pharmacy as a pharmacy assistant.

- In high school, you painted houses over summer break for spending money.

This all sounds pretty good to me. Even at an early age, you were quite the entrepreneur. How do you feel about your experience?

On a typical résumé, one would list jobs, dates, and experience highlights, but you do not want a typical résumé—you want to catch the attention of the company and get noticed. Have fun with this piece. After all, if a company does not appreciate creativity, they may not appreciate you. As stated earlier, you can find a sample résumé in Attachment 2, but let's just have some fun and get a bit bold by writing your professional experience in a format that I guarantee will gain attention.

13

Professional/Educational Experience

State University   **Sept 2007–May 2011**

- BS, Chemistry, Graduated with high honors in **Top 10 percent** of my class
- Achieved the **Crystal Beaker award**, a recognition of top talent in chemistry
- Awarded laboratory assistant position, **instructing others** in lab technique
- Vice president of Chemistry Club, **initiating** monthly meetings on special topics

Employment History   **Summer Work**

- **Earned** the duties of pharmacy assistant at Pills-4-U pharmacy
- Assisted the pharmacist and retail manager while **developing** great customer rapport
- **Designed** drug inventory files for pharmacist, a computer project on the weekends
- **Developed** stock orders with the local distributor, inputting SKUs in the system
- **Requested** back for three consecutive summers by chief pharmacist
- As a high school student, **managed** my own painting company in summers for extra cash

Okay, we are finished. Too wild for you? Well, it might be for some, but I personally would look at this résumé before others, and it's probably first in the stack on my desk. The reason behind this is that the points chosen for emphasis are action oriented and are active in voice, that is, they show determination, confidence, and some assertiveness to the reader.

You have to live in your own skin, as the saying goes, so go with whatever style makes you comfortable and feels professional at the same time. I am illustrating how to catch the reviewer's attention. There are probably as many different ideas as there are styles, but work out what you feel is good, and go for it. Go comfortably into this phase, and focus on the essentials. The content will sell your new employer.

The Cardinal Rules for Résumé Building

1. Be clear on what you are looking for in a job.

2. State what you have done with a positive and enthusiastic tone.

3. Recognize that *Pinocchio* is a great children's story, but never lie or even stretch the truth on your résumé. If your nose grows, the job goes!

Note

Do not embellish anything you have done, as it is discoverable, as lawyers might phrase it. In lay terms, this simply means that if a fact is stretched or exaggerated, it can be checked for accuracy, and many times companies do check for accuracy of statements. As an example, if you were nominated to head your chemistry club, but declined, it is better to say it than to embellish it by saying you were the head of the club. If you assisted students on an ad hoc basis, but not as a laboratory assistant, say that, too. I had an excellent employee who stated she had graduated from a prominent state university. After several years, a company that did résumé checks on all employees to match skills with employer needs acquired us. They found out that this person attended the university but did not graduate. She was six hours short of her degree. Lucky for her, she kept her job. Needless to say, I was embarrassed and dismayed. We remained associates, but on a slightly different level. Trust in the workplace is paramount to success, and if you start with a truthful résumé, you march down the right path—the only path.

Cover Letters Are a Waste of Time, Unless You...

Most of the cover letters I have received over the years were worthless to me, even those from executives applying to join my staff as department heads. A great cover letter captures the attention of the reader and offers suggestions about what that individual can do for the supervisor and the company. In Attachment 3, you can find an example of a good cover letter, but let's discuss it briefly before we go on to doing our research. The résumé is the foundation of your house, but the cover letter permits you the freedom to decorate it, and it is important to focus on this feature.

At this early stage of your career, a résumé is somewhat generic in structure, that is, it describes what you want and what you have done. It does not address what you will do for a company, the cover letter does. This is your time to sell yourself!

Assume your prospective company does a lot of work in quantitative chemistry, for example, determining the amount of a contaminant in a sample of incoming raw materials. What should you include in your cover letter?

- If you were a wizard in quantitative analysis in college and were able to run recovery studies of 99 percent or better, while others struggled to recover better than 95 percent, provide these statistics.

- If you did graduate-level course work in quant, as that was your thing, emphasize your love for this specific branch of chemistry in the letter.

Most importantly, you must demonstrate your willingness and desire for the position. What phrases make employers smile?

- "This position is very exciting to me as I really want to work in this area of chemistry."

- "I would happily consider overtime, nights, or week-ends if it helped the company."

It is mandatory to let prospective companies know you want to work for them, as there are many applicants but only one of you, and you are the one of interest, correct? By this point in the process, I hope you are able to give a resounding yes to the previous question.

Finally, personalize cover letters to the company for which you are applying. Do not make it look like a mass-produced form letter. Everyone, even prospective employers, likes to feel your love and interest. Take the time to research something you can say about the company in your letter. For example:

- The Arsenic Residue Recovery Project is of high personal interest. I believe the work in this area is helpful to all people.

- The opportunity to work with the Department of Health and Human Services is a challenge I welcome, and it will help me bring value to the company.

If you specifically reference how your skills will benefit the company, it will be more favorably accepted than simply saying you are an excellent bench chemist. How about this instead? "I am an excellent bench chemist in quantitative chemistry analysis. Plus, I have completed advanced work on recovery of hard-to-detect contaminants." Better? I think so.

Review Step 2 of 8
What have you discovered thus far?

1. **Don't shortchange yourself on the time spent on this section.** It can take hours to perfect a résumé that makes you stand out. Spend the time! Type it out in different formats to see how you react. It will also serve to solidify your thinking about your background.

2. **Start with yourself to build a selling résumé.** Emphasize your abilities to help your supervisor and her hiring company.[3]

3. **Personalize your résumé to the target company.** If you can drop bits of information about your skills in relation to the job, you win.

4. **Relax.** You have more experience than you think. Take the time to define what you have done well in your college and pre-college years if you feel the accomplishments warrant sharing.

5. **Don't embellish or lie.** No, no, no, Pinocchio!

6. **Recognize that personalized cover letters sell.** They don't just tell. The next step is all about the research necessary to win the job race.

7. **Demonstrate your desire for the job.** Ask for the interview. Sell yourself!

---

3 You will be employed by the company, but never forget, if you specifically address the concerns of the hiring supervisor, it weighs heavily in the supervisor's decision. And he or she will hire you, not the company.

Congratulations! You have completed 25 percent of the race, and I feel like you are ahead of the pack. Do you?

Step 3
Research and Development

This step implies learning the most you can from the material easily generated on the web, through networking, or other outside resources and then developing that information into a real lead. I have an opinion on the many types of social networks available today. Even though you can add your résumé and qualifications quite easily to any number of sites, general or specific, these searches are usually generic.[4] You will compete with thousands of global applicants who inundate the very same sites you are tapping into with your résumé.

Many HR departments will look at these sites frequently, but with a limited search radius.[5] For the most part, these companies will not pay for relocation, so, if you are outside their radius, they will ignore you. Generally, they will not take the time to discover whether you are willing to relocate at your expense to get the position. They call it "geographic screening," but a more apt term may be "geographic preclusion." You get exactly what you put into a job

---

4 Most first-time job hunters are not members of organized Web-based communities pertinent to job sites reflecting their interests.

5 Radius is the generally accepted commuting time and distance from the company site for entry-level positions. Generally, this distance is approximately twenty-five to fifty miles.

search, so I highly recommend the personal approach. After all, you are selling yourself, not just casting into a sea of innumerable résumés hoping for a nibble from a prospective company.

Discovering Potential Employers

Most companies have a ton of information available on their websites.

A website for smaller companies may include the following features:

- Home page describing what they do
- Products and services tab defining the individual products and services available
- Contact tab providing information for e-mailing/calling/faxing the company

In contrast, larger companies will have more extensive sites, usually including tiered drop-down windows. I have chosen to look at a large software conglomerate as an example. I will call them Software-R-Us.

At the top of the home page, the company provides the following drop-down menu. Areas of importance are defined below.

Products	**Buy Now**	**Downloads & Trial**	**Partner & Customer**
Solutions	**Security/ Updates**	**Support**	**About Us**

To begin, browse the company's range of products so you can familiarize yourself with their offerings, but before you get too involved with products or technology, skip ahead to the About Us tab. Under that tab, you see a bullet identified as Investor Relations. It looks like this:

Company	Financials	Annual Reports	SEC Filings	Events
Stock Info	Investor Services	Corporate Officers	Contacts	

Here you will find information that is pertinent to your search. You should spend a good deal of your research time here to discover information that other first-time job seekers may skip. Notice, I did not mention development yet; right now you are in the research phase. Let's get started by looking at the various sections that follow. Each one is interesting in itself, but don't worry, I have indicated those where you should spend the majority of your time.

Company: This section provides a general overview of the company, its structure, location, and purpose.

Financials: This area focuses on many facets of the health of the company, such as earnings, for interested investors. You can find some common definitions of financial terms in Attachment 4: Glossary 101 of Business Terms.

> ## Note
>
> Financial terms are sometimes even confusing to finance people, as they consist of ratios designed to judge the health of a company. As mentioned previously, I have provided a glossary of terms that gives some direction on definitions; however, it is anything but inclusive of all the terms and mechanisms that people use to judge companies. This is not all that important to you currently, but you should be familiar with the basics, as you will see it ties to the development section. (I have provided P&L [profit and loss] and balance sheet definitions in the attachment.)

Annual Reports: This is the company's summation of how the previous year compared to what they had forecasted and sells futures to their investors. It is extremely detailed, with financials, news of the company, and reviews of the year by the chairman and CEO. You can peruse previous annual reports and gain information on a cursory basis, but your goal is to get a job, not invest in the company.

SEC Filings: This material focuses on the transactions the company and its officers have made. This is important only directionally. For example, if you notice that many of the officers have divested their stock holdings or are trending toward divestiture, it would beg the question of company stability and confidence going forward.

Note

If you have access to someone such as a friend or family member who works in the finance area of a different company, it might be beneficial for you to ask him or her for a brief review of your target company from a financial perspective and keep his or her analysis in your data file, PDA, and so forth.

Events: This simply states all the events the company or its representatives have participated in over the year(s). Usually, the more active a company is in global or local events, the more aggressively it is marketing itself, and that can be a good thing.

Stock Information: In this area, it is probably best to focus on the trending of the stock over time, as this is the easiest to find and understand. A lot of information is in this subcategory, but don't get too hung up on trying to understand it in detail. Again, if interested, ask someone financially fluent for his or her opinion.

Investor Services: Just skip this section. It really doesn't affect your job decision.

Corporate Governance: This is more fascinating than helpful. It is fun to see who is in charge and where they recently held positions. It has vision, policy, and more chapters than *Moby Dick*.[6] So, unless you are an information freak, don't spend a lot of time.

---

6 135 Chapters, Moby Dick, last modified July 28, 2011, http://en.wikipedia.org/wiki/mobi-dick

Contacts: For you, this is the focus section. Companies make it easy to contact them, as they list their addresses, phone and fax numbers, e-mail addresses, and, in most cases, direct links to the HR department.

What Do You Look for in a Company? (Development)

Okay, I have filled your head with material, but how do you use it meaningfully? Now is time to develop what you have learned. Let's put it into chart form.

Our chemistry grad wants to live in Chicago and work in the pharmaceutical or biotech business as a bench chemist. I have chosen eight parameters, but the list can be shorter or longer. That is a personal decision. I chose these eight as they are basic to everyone thinking about new employment, so I recommend you use them to your advantage. To best utilize the chart, rank each company with your top preference first and then your second preference, but, keep flexibility in mind. You are now just looking to gain experience. This decision does not span a lifetime. It just provides a needed start.

EMPLOYMENT ESSENTIALS College Edition

	Company			
	A	**B**	**C**	**Ranking by Preference**
Location (city)	Chicago	Skokie	St. Charles	A
Company size (number of employees)	5,000	15	500	A
Field of focus	Pharmaceuticals	Biotech	Contract research	B
Prestige	Forbes 500	Start-up, three years in business	Private, thirty-five years in business	A, C
Job availability	Quantitative chemistry and quality control	Bench chemistry in many areas	Routine validation testing	A, B
Commuting	Live in city (public transportation)	Five-mile commute	Two-mile commute	C
Cost of living	High rental cost, possibility for roommates, car unnecessary	Steep apartment rent, easy commute, car necessary	Apartment rent more reasonable, could commute by bike on nice days, local shopping easy	C
Lifestyle	All excellent for arts, sports, and nightlife	Laid back, easy to access city by train	More country, open with many outdoor parks and attractions	B

In this brief example, it looks like Company A is a good fit for you, followed by either company B or C. Company A probably has more opportunities because of its size. You can make up some of what you will suffer in living expense via public transportation, as you would not immediately need/have a car, car insurance, fuel, parking, and toll costs each month.

Note

At this stage of your career, gaining experience is more important than location or preference. Remember, you can change the decision you make today once you get some experience under your belt. Accepting employment is no longer a commitment for life. Many workers today change jobs every eighteen to twenty-four months, and the industry no longer frowns upon it. We are a very mobile society, so expect to move a few times in your career. If you embrace that up-front, it will not shock you in the future when you decide to relocate due to family, marriage, new opportunities, or anything else that drives your decisions.

What Role Do Recruiters Play in All of This?

I love recruiters. In fact, some of my best friends are recruiters, but I do not recommend using a recruiter for a starting position. There are recruiters who will offer services to entry-level candidates, but, oftentimes, you can get this same information via college or civic placement offices. The reason few recruiters work for entry-level positions is that the fee for service is quite low, and most companies do not want to pay any fee for an entry-level individual. For your information, recruiters generally work to find candidates for companies for a fee, paid by the company. As you progress in your career, you will find that some recruiters work on retained searches, meaning they have exclusive rights and responsibilities. A retained search is generally limited to top-tier executive employees, but it can vary. Recruiters are important people to know and to develop relationships with, as they provide an extremely important service to all industries. Over time, make an effort to find out which recruiters are best in your specific industry.

Additional Resources for Job Attainment

Job fairs and state and local employment offices can also be a huge help to you. You are going to find many job-posting sites (Monster.com), but these sites only list jobs that companies post.[7] I advocate using these sites, but remember that many companies in your area will not post publicly, so doing your own research is paramount to your success. Some of the greatest jobs are never publicly posted. That is why it is important to cold-call and network. Plus, very few of your competitors will have this information, so you will be submitting a focused résumé, not a generic one of hundreds or even thousands. You can also network with friends and family members within your industry of choice. Don't be timid. Ask for help. Networking opens doors, but

---

7 Monster.com furnishes great information on jobs, résumé building, and so forth.

only you can close them. In the next section, we will discuss the big connect. This will help you put the proper focus on gaining the first interview.

Review Step 3 of 8
What have you discovered thus far?

1. **Do take the time necessary in researching.** It is like a career savings account. It will come back to you with multifold benefits.

2. **Utilize all tools available.** A gamut of tools today can help you research your job opportunities. Focus on a few, but rely on yourself.

3. **Take command of your own search.** Actively doing the groundwork furthers your education in job hunting.

4. **Research and prioritize.** Utilize your own priority matrix. Define your desires and needs for the short term.

5. **Make decisions for today.** You are not indentured to a company. Once you gain experience, you can change jobs, locale, or even professions.

6. **Recognize that recruiters are great, but not for today.** Gaining experience and a good recruiter can pay big dividends, but experience first and recruiting second.

7. **Network with those you know and trust.** Ask for help in your search or in explaining pieces of the process from those you know and trust.

8. **Go for it!**

You have now taken charge of your situation! Sit back and take a break, as you have accomplished a ton. You are much more in control of your job hunt than the paper-hangers who feel good about sending résumés to the universe.

Step 4
The Big Connect

How Do I Get the Attention of Prospective Employers?

You are more prepared than you think, as you have a ton of information at this point. You are now ready to make some contacts. Let's review what you know at this stage:

1. You have defined your goals and tested them for realism.

2. You have decided what job you would like to perform for your new company.

3. You know your résumé is stellar, you have learned what you need in your cover letter, and it sells.

4. You have looked at geographic preferences and potential employers in that area.

5. You have had a chance to review important information about prospective companies by utilizing the tools available on websites of interest. Keep a file for each company you investigate so you can quickly assess the differences and advantages each offers.

6. You have accessed (or know where to access) free help in finding opportunities in your community.

Now is the time to connect. This section is the easiest by far, and it will also be the briefest, as it is relatively straightforward.

Go back to number 4 above and to your chart of companies. Start with your first choice and do the following:

1. Get the contact information through the website or whatever source you used to find the company.

2. Write a personalized cover letter for your résumé that stresses your interest in attaining a position with the company. Throw in a few facts that you have learned about the company to show that you have done your homework.

3. Mention the company's name in your letter.

4. Ask for the opportunity to speak with or meet with a representative at the company's convenience. Let them know that your schedule is open.

5. Attach your résumé and cover letter to an e-mail. The e-mail should be brief and concise stating that you are applying for a position with the company and that you have attached your cover letter and résumé. Sign it with Best regards, and your name. There is no reason to add more as you have covered that in your cover letter. Keep all correspondence in a file by individual company on your computer so you can readily access all communications. Most of the time, the HR department re-

ceives your résumé and cover letter. Now you are ready for that first phone discussion.

Note

Once you send your inquiry to the company, don't wait more than three to five days for a response. Call the company's HR department and ask to speak to someone about your recent employment inquiry. Write down the names of the people you speak with, and keep them in your file. The HR administrator gets many calls, and he or she appreciates those people who find him or her important enough to remember names.

If you get a negative or put-off response ("I will see that Ms. Bertrand gets your résumé"), ask what procedure they use for notifying applicants if there is a chance to further the process. If you get the "We-will-keep-it-on-file" routine, say "Thank you" and call back in another week. Sometimes, the squeaky wheel gets the grease. You can also resend the résumé and cover letter in a week or two, but preface it with a statement that you are simply making sure they received the first submission. Persistence is the key to success.

Does Networking Help?

Probably nothing is as good as a reference, period. Friends, family, social contacts, church members, or anyone who is connected to a company or industry may be able to give your name to others and have that eventually filter back to hiring managers. I personally have hired many employees that colleagues, oftentimes in other industries, referenced.

Remember, you are selling now, and you should take advantage of every lead opportunity. Send your résumés to any contact you have, and ask them to pass it on to the proper sources.

Social networking on professional networks such as LinkedIn and Facebook can be extremely useful for finding people connected with others in your field. Look in your college alumni association, and find those who come from your field. They would be excellent targets for sending résumés. Remember; explain that you found them through the alumni association. Ask if they know of any employment opportunities applicable to your background. Oftentimes, people are reluctant to recommend an individual they do not know. You should not ask for that. Simply ask if they are familiar with positions requiring your background. People help people.

Knocking on Doors Is Not out of Style

If you are interested in companies in your area, put on a decent outfit, and hand-carry your cover letter and résumé to the company of interest. Go to the front desk, and ask to speak with someone in HR who covers employment. They may ask you to fill out an application, and, if you're lucky, they may even speak with you. Job hunters with college degrees do this so infrequently that many miss opportunities for direct contact with companies within driving distance. Don't drive by a job opportunity. Stop and inquire.

Surfing for Action, Not Fun

I am not redoing the research section, but this is so important that I thought a little redundancy would be okay. No matter how many potential employers you find for prospective employment, you must keep looking for new opportunities. Think of this as your job funnel. The more opportunities within your funnel, the better the chances are that one will fall out in your favor. Even if you find that you are getting to a first or second interview, do not stop searching, as anything can happen in the job world. It is wise not to put all your money on one outcome. I have often seen that jobs open on Monday were frozen on Friday, so don't get trapped in that game. Keep your surfing serious.

Great waves today! Job surfing is wild and really kicks up the job adrenaline.

Review Step 4 of 8
What have you discovered thus far?

1. **Gather your information.** You have created files on the companies you are targeting.

2. **Review your targeted companies.** Go back to your chart and create personalized résumés and cover letters.

3. **Send and follow up.** Contact and continue to follow up on your submissions.

4. **Network.** Build your pipeline of opportunities by soliciting others to help you find opportunities through their networks.

5. **Knock on some doors**. Actively pursuing positions with easily accessible companies in your vicinity can't hurt, and you may be the only one with the foresight to do so.

6. **Surf for action.** Continue contacting and discovering opportunities. As in number 3 above, building the pipeline will increase your chances. This is where social networking can help you gain exposure.

Great job! You have now sent several inquiries to your companies of interest, and you are anticipating the soon-to-come calls from your targeted, prospective employers.

Step 5
The One and Only First Interview

How to Prepare through Research and Fact-Finding

No, you are not going backward. You have read this before, but it is worth reiteration. In Step 3, you learned about researching and developing the information concerning prospective employers. Do not get caught in the unprepared mode. The following example will say it all.

Example

You have researched several companies, submitted your résumé, and tailored your cover letter to their specific sites. It is Tuesday afternoon, and you have just had lunch. You thought you would begin researching new opportunities and then go to your spin class. The phone rings, and it is Company A. Your dream job is on the other end of the phone, and you are excited. No, you are over the edge with excitement. An HR representative asks if you have time to speak to her about your résumé. Oh, wow! Oh no!

Critical Advice

If you are unprepared for the call, it is best to say you that you were just leaving for a class but really want to speak with them. Ask if it would be possible to set up a time to speak, even if only a few hours from that time, the next day, or any other time at her convenience. It is certainly better to be ready to take the call, but even veterans can be caught off guard. Obviously, don't take the call if you are in a noisy area. Call back.

Why this technique? You have not yet reached professional status in interviewing, and you do not want to be unprepared. Use the following strategy:

- If she states it is acceptable and names a time, you are golden.

- If she says, "Well, I will just try you again later," indicate you will miss the class and take the interview, as nothing is more important than this job.

Is this double-talk? No! Delaying an unannounced call is a good option, as your best chance lies in stacking everything to your favor. One school of thought says you should take the call, as it may not come again, but believe me, if you can get it rescheduled, you will likely be more successful, as preparation breeds success.

Note

Keep files on each company to which you have submitted résumés. Have them in a place that is easily accessible if you are forced into a call. Last, once you have prepared your files, review them often so you are on top of your game when the big call comes, as such calls seem to never come at opportune times. Be prepared because you can then relax and comfortably take calls as they come.

Talking with HR Screeners

The HR departments in many companies have screeners, people who are paid to contact and initiate the first screening interview with prospective employees. In smaller companies, this person is usually the hiring manager, but both conversations are basic.

The company's goal for this call is to ferret out several candidates, those who are optimistic, articulate, and somewhat informed about the company. The calls usually last from thirty to sixty minutes. Your responsibility is to be as prepared for the target company as possible. Use the following guidelines:

- Be alert.

- Listen to the questions before responding.

- Try to make it a general conversation, not just a Q&A session, as your personality comes across in dialogue, not in Q&A.

What Will They Ask Me? And How Can I Be Ready to Respond?

To start, you should have immediate answers for some typical questions.[8]

1. How did you find us? Why did you select our company for employment?

2. Tell me about your educational experience and how it relates to the job of interest.

3. What courses did you most/least enjoy while in school?

4. What do you know about our company and the area (city/location) surrounding the company?

5. What do you like to do in your free time?

6. Are you available to work evenings or weekends if necessary?

7. What contribution do you feel you can make to the company over other applicants with similar backgrounds?

8. Why should we select you over others for this job?

9. What are your strengths and weaknesses that we should consider?

Ad infinitum!

---

8 A sample Q&A is available in Attachment 5: Sample Questions and Answers.

What Do I Ask Them? I Don't Have a Clue What to Ask to Be Truthful.

How funny really! Most people don't have a clue. Even some of the higher-level executives I have interviewed in the last several years have fumbled on this one. Considering this guide is primarily for new entrants to the job market, the really tough questions will be omitted, but you still want to be prepared and knowledgeable. Included are some examples of questions about your prospective job and employer that are totally fair game. Don't overwhelm the interviewer, as he or she is interviewing you. It can be irritating when he or she has ten people to call in a single day and you ask too many questions. Feel it out. If he or she seems receptive, ask all of the following. If not, let him or her know you have many questions but will be happy to ask them on the next interview. (Yeah, it is positive and not too aggressive, and it is a trial close.) Trial close is a term frequently used to ask for the job or next event without blatantly calling it out. It is a good technique as it helps you determine the position of the interviewer. Legitimate questions for your interviewer include

1. What is the job description for this position? Could I receive a copy?

2. Generally, what hours are expected? And would I be an hourly worker (nonexempt) or salaried (exempt)? Do not get hung up on the answer to this question. Federal laws dictate guidelines for hourly versus salaried

employees. If interested, you can check into the laws dictating the policies.[9]

3. Who would I report to? This could be a supervisor, manager of section, manager of laboratory, VP of quality, and so forth. Don't ask directly for the person's name until the next interview. It isn't necessary and may falsely show prejudice on your part through gender, nationality and so forth.

4. How many others with my background currently work in this department?

5. What is your process for hiring?

6. What must I do to bring this to the next level, and what is the time frame?

Close the First Step, Not the Deal

Always leave them with a positive impression. "Thank you so much for contacting me. I hope I have answered all your questions thoroughly, and I appreciate your time in answering mine. I am really excited about testing bovine sputum eight hours a day, and I look forward to grabbing the bull by the horns." Pun intended, but let the screener know at the end of the conversation that you look forward to taking this to the next level.

9 Most jobs are governed under the Fair Labor Standard Act (FLSA), but some are not. Check the FLSA policy for your company if you are interested in learning more about exempt versus nonexempt.

Note

Make sure you capture the interviewer's name and phone number. Make sure he or she knows all the ways to contact you, and follow up immediately with a handwritten thank-you note or e-mail.[10] Call back in three days to see if you can provide anything else. I'm sure you have all heard the expression "One attracts more bees with honey than with vinegar." You can't be too positive or too nice on this phone interview, because, if you are not, you don't need to read Step 6 of this guide. Go back to Step 1.

Review Step 5 of 8
What have you discovered thus far?

1. **Be prepared 24-7 for the first call**. It is great if you can be prepared to take an unannounced call, but, if you are not confident, try to reschedule with just enough time to get ready. Even an hour will help.

2. **Practice for the HR screener.** As mentioned, you can find a guide of common questions in the attachments. Some are listed in the body above. Practice them until you deliver fluently without sounding canned.

---

10 I like handwritten notes. They are special, but it is a greener world, and e-mail is acceptable.

3. **Practice your questions.** These do not have to be memorized. Simply indicate that you have some questions and have written them down. It shows organization and forethought.

4. **Close the first step.** Your goal is to get to the next step, not close on the job. So pull back on the reins and close the screening interview.

You must feel great about your progress, and you should. By following the process, you have successfully handled the first big step through direct contact with the company. Take the afternoon off, and enjoy yourself. It is quite an accomplishment, and you will only get better with time.

Step 6
Day of Reckoning:
The Face-to-Face Interview

The Answer Is Less Important Than the Question!

How can this be? This seems paradoxical to most, but it has a deeper meaning than what appears on the surface. I am stressing that you should listen and listen well. Experienced and inexperienced job seekers make this mistake routinely. They do not fully listen to the question, as they are already formulating answers in their heads.

Note

It is entirely proper and shows your level of interest to ask the interviewer whether you can take notes during the interview. I have had less than half of new entrants to the job market ask me that question. I certainly allowed them to take notes, as it indicated to me that they were of an organized nature. Don't write a book during the interview, but take notes in your shorthand that will allow you to remember the conversations or interviewer's body language.

For example, an interviewer asks you, "What do you feel your biggest contribution to our company would be?" Many new entrants to the job market freeze on this, even if they have rehearsed, as it seems the right answer is escaping them. My advice is to

- Pause.

- Take a few seconds to organize your thoughts.

- Remember what you have studied, as you are prepared for this.

- Say, "That is a good question. Let me think for a minute."

The last step shows you are a well-balanced person and prone to thinking something out before answering.

Let's just explore this one question: "What do you feel your biggest contribution to our company would be?" First, what is the motivation behind such a question? Is there a right answer? What is the best answer?

The motivation is often multifold. How do you react? Are you confident? And, finally, what do you think you bring to the company? Remember, most likely, several people are interviewing for this position, so you want to be on your game.

Is there a right answer? No, this is an open-ended question that gives you a chance to perform at your best. The quality of your response is equal to or greater in importance than the answer itself.

What is the best answer? The best answer again requires some thought, but, if you have prepared, you are ready in spades to nail this one to the desk!

Example

A good friend of mine has a son at a well-known and highly respected university in the New York City Area. She told me he would react by saying he had leadership ability, tenacity, honesty, and team experience, along with the requisite course work necessary to do the job.[11]

An answer of this caliber is excellent, but not totally descriptive. He could improve upon this answer, for example:

"I believe I bring many qualities that will benefit this company. At the University I learned leadership through organizing and driving the agenda for all chemistry club projects in my senior year, gaining experience in management of both people and projects. I am tenacious. Once I begin or have an assignment given to me, I don't let go until it is completed, and my work energy is off the charts. I am an honest person, and I would rather lose the opportunity for this job than to say something that embellishes the truth about my experience or me. I learned the importance of teamwork in my free time activities. I took up flying as a hobby and the work involved in earning my pilot's license has definitely made me aware of the importance of teamwork and interaction. I learned that the pilot doesn't make the plane fly. He only flies it. The engineers, mechanics,

---

11 Used with permission

ground crew, trainers, and air traffic controllers make the planes fly. I was simply part of the team. Last but not least, my coursework in chemistry combined with my tenure as a lab assistant definitely qualifies me for this role as a bench chemist for your company."

Knock their socks off, candidate. I guarantee the interviewer will be impressed because this interviewee has prepared in advance, not just for the specific question, but for a general response as to why he or she is qualified. This type of preparation will almost guarantee that you will be invited back, but you must practice, and we deal with that step later.

How to Answer a Majority of the Questions in Advance of the Interview

I recently read a well-known, respected author stating that preparing for interviews with preprinted questions was a waste of time because you never know what the interviewer might ask. I have since stopped reading that author. Only one thing comes out of the back of a bull, and, if you believe that practice questions are a waste of time, you are stepping in it. In Attachment 5, I have included a thorough list of questions that will more than likely be asked.

Note

Think of the questions as a guideline. First, answer my questions as you would hope to answer in the interview. Then get creative. I urge you to use literary license to edit the questions with a different slant or tone. Even alter the questions altogether. Of course, the aforementioned author is correct. No one can predict what the interviewer may ask, as everyone is different and skilled at varying levels, but not practicing with a set of bona fide questions is a cardinal mistake. If you choose to not follow the suggestions I make in the next few sections, just stop reading, and I wish you luck in your job pursuit. I feel that strongly about what follows.

Practice Makes Passable; Role-Playing Makes Perfect

Not only does role-playing make perfect, it gives you time to enhance your answering ability in as close to a real-life interview as possible. You can role-play easily, as I have included a mock interview in Attachment 6. For those of you unfamiliar with role-playing, it is simply two or more people taking sides, one asking the questions and the other answering. Ask your best friend, a family member, or even a favorite teacher to help you with this. If no one is available, it's no problem, as you can simply play both roles. Read the question, and then respond. It isn't quite as good as a two-way conversation, but it does help you practice.

Note

It has long been recognized that practicing in front of a mirror for a speech is a good tool, as you can see how you appear in the delivery. This holds true for interviewing if no one is able to assist. With today's tools and phones, you can probably video yourself and stream it to your computer so you can see how you react. Make sure you use body language properly, for example, sit up straight, look the interviewer in the eyes, and smile. You can discover body language tips and courses in many areas on the Internet, if desired.

Getting the Next Interview by Closing the First

You have done a remarkable job during the first face-to-face interview, but you are not finished yet. Here is a small list of must-dos to gain the next interview and secure your new position. Now, let's close the face-to-face interview. We will assume the interview portion is over.

1. When the interviewer asks if you have any additional questions and you have already asked the questions I recommend in Attachment 5, then ask or state the following:

   a. Thank the interviewer for his or her time. Ask if there is anything that he or she asked that you have not clearly addressed and say that you would be happy to go back and clarify if needed.

b. Ask what the next steps are and if you could have his or her business card.

c. State that you can be reached any time at the appropriate contact numbers listed on your résumé, and include your e-mail address so nothing can impede contact with you.

4. Ask for the job by simply saying you are very excited about this position and you believe you qualify through your background. Indicate you want to work for this company. You will be asking for the position many times before you're finished.

5. Don't stand up until the interviewer does, but, once he or she does, the interview is definitely over. Don't say anything but "Thank you" and "I look forward to speaking again soon." Look him or her in the eyes when shaking hands and leaving. Maintain some level of control right to the end.

Without levity, I would never have lasted more than thirty years in the working environment. I must tell you a story.

• I once conducted an interview with a well-qualified potential candidate from a highly regarded university. An articulate man, he was dressed nicely and answered my questions about his background with a great degree of confidence. When we stood to leave, I shook his hand and said I enjoyed meeting him and that we would be in contact with him within a few days. He then said, in a much exaggerated manner, "Don't believe a word those b------- say about me when checking references. I did not have a drug problem. I just couldn't sleep for a couple months, and I looked and felt terrible. They are just trying to mess with my life."

How funny, I couldn't wait to tell my colleagues of this story, and, of course, I checked the references just to see what they had to say. That story would probably be a best seller, but I leave that for my retirement years.

Obviously, I'm emphasizing that you should leave with a professional exit. It's no time for jokes, stories, asking about the family, telling about your snorkeling trip during spring break, or anything else. Just turn and leave.

By the way, as you leave, thank the administrator, if the interviewer has one, and the receptionist. As before with the phone interview, send a handwritten thank-you note or e-mail, and restate the reasons why you believe you are highly qualified. Then ask for the chance to go to the next step.

Dressing for Success, Not the Red Carpet

I do not want to go back in history, when dressing for success meant a suit and tie for a man and a business suit for a woman. Come on, I am not that old! I mean you should dress for the occasion. Prior to the first face-to-face interview, it is totally proper to ask what business attire is appropriate for the job you are seeking. If you are interviewing for a position and you feel it warrants a suit, then wear one, but I wouldn't show up in a designer brand with more jewelry than the queen, no matter what the job. It does not pay to be overdressed in almost any situation.

Many businesses today are business casual, meaning slacks, shirts, skirts, pants, sweaters, and so forth, but not jeans. If they feel it is important to tell you to dress down, as you will be touring a laboratory filled with caustic materials, then go ahead and wear a relaxed outfit, but I still would not wear jeans to the interview. This applies to all, whether you are the chemist right out of college or applying for a market research position. I suggest sticking to business casual as the minimum clothing requirement. A jacket is never inappropriate, as it dresses up the outfits for men and women without overdressing. Allow me another story concerning my reference to the red carpet.

- I once interviewed a young woman who had a college degree and spent a few months selling cosmetics in a retail outlet. She was trained in the sciences and wanted a job in sales with my medical diagnostics company. Well, she was shown to my office, and I couldn't believe my eyes. I won't describe the outfit, as it would be inappropriate, but, suffice it to say, it was inappropriate dress. How did I know that? Every person in the office passed by my door while she was interviewing. She had fine jewelry. It was too much and too nice, as it almost became a distraction.

I think you get the picture. Get real. Don't overdress for your position, whatever the role. Look neat, clean, and ready to work, not shoot the next scene from a Hollywood blockbuster. It is also understood that you shouldn't show up looking disheveled. It is definitely worth a professional cleaning and pressing for whatever outfit you choose to wear!

Review Step 6 of 8
What have you discovered thus far?

1. **Listen before you speak.** Make sure you listen to and understand the question being asked of you. Don't anticipate a response in advance.

2. **Contemplate the motivation for the question.** It will help you formulate a thorough answer, but also keeps you from rambling.

3. **Practice your responses through role-playing.** A few hours per day of role-playing will make you an expert in fielding questions. **Gain the next interview by closing the first face-to-face interview properly.** Once again, give it your all, but don't assume it will come down to one interview. In many companies today, they want to be careful with selections, as they are given fewer selections due to budgeting.

4. **Dress appropriately.** Nothing more needs to be said in this area.

You have completed 75 percent of the process, and you are ready for the job. Congratulations! The next few steps will get you a paycheck. I am excited for you and hope you feel the same about your progress thus far.

Step 7
The Next Interview Could Be Your Last, and That Is Your Goal

Follow Up After the First Interview

Okay, you have nailed the first interview, and you feel good about it. The interviewer seemed impressed and said she really enjoyed speaking with you and you would be hearing from them soon. This leaves three options, but you want only one, correct? The options are:

1. They invite you back for a last interview.

2. They indicate they are still looking and will get back to you, and perhaps...

3. They offer you the position.

Options one and three are the most desirable; the second option signals you must enact Step 7 immediately. There's no time to waste. The following are now the cardinal rules for progression.

1. **Study your notes and put them into a saved document for referral while preparing for the final interview.** I assume you have taken my advice and made notes of your conversation during the first interview. Use your own form of shorthand. If the interviewer

seems to like your answer, smiles, and writes something down on a legal pad, I would just annotate it something like this: Impressed with lab assistant job ☆. As a recent college grad, it may appear to be somewhat less than what you are capable of doing, but it takes only a second to write, and you will remember to focus on it. Of course, if the interviewer throws a pen across the room after you answer a question and asks you to leave, no note would be necessary. Please go back to Step 1 for serious review.

2. **Review what was said for about thirty minutes and remember how you answered the questions.** Do this while the interview discussion is still fresh in your mind. Write a summary of the discussion so you will answer the questions in your next interview in the same manner or even in an improved manner the second time. Be aware that oftentimes questions are repeated in successive interviews to determine whether your answers are consistent.

3. **Create a handwritten, businesslike thank-you note or e-mail.** Then follow the same policy as suggested previously. Emphasize your strong points and why they make you a strong contender for this job. You must remember the next point above all.

4. **Ask for the job**. Just come right out and tell the interviewer that you feel very positive about the company and personnel you have met with and you would love to work for this company. It's neat, clean, and easy to do,

but it adds a lot to a personal note. Okay, relax a bit. You are almost there!

The next section covers writing a personal plan for what you feel you would do or accomplish if hired. If you feel the interviewer was highly interested or expresses after the first interview that he or she believes you have a great background, consider sending the personal plan along with your thank-you note. It would be a knockout punch. The plan is fun to create, and I can almost assure that you will be one of few entry-level candidates that will do this.

Come Back with a Plan That Highlights Your Future Contribution

Note

If you are being highly considered, meeting others in the department in which you will work could happen in the first interview, so be prepared even in that first face-to-face interview to meet your soon-to-be peers. More than likely, for an entry-level position, your peers will not interview you. They will just get an opportunity to meet you.

Okay, let's get started on your plan. For managerial, senior, and executive positions, this is critical and expected, but even an entry-level person can have a plan of what he or she will do once the job is his or hers. We are going to create exactly that. Bring the plan with you, and, before the second interview starts, tell the interviewer that you have penned some ideas of what you feel is important for you to do if you get the position. He or she may or may not look at it, but don't be concerned either way. Just do it. If you send it with the thank-you note after the first interview, start the second interview by asking if the interviewer received your plan. Be prepared to reiterate it if asked, and, again, bring a copy with you.

In the Beginning: You and Only You Have Created a Plan[12]

The plan should be succinct. That is, it should list your activities once a job has been attained, aside from the company's training plans.[13] The plan should consist of the following:

- Start with a preemptive close. "In anticipation of being hired, I have prepared the following list of actions that I will take to ensure a rapid growth curve for the position."

- State that you are excited about the training program and look forward to participating.

- Indicate that you have studied for the last several years, so you plan to work on your own time to review company policies and manuals that surround the job.

---

12 A sample plan format is available in Attachment 9.

13 Caution: Do not offer suggestions or criticisms of anything you saw during the last interview. Just offer the positive things you will do on your own to augment the company's training. There will be time enough in the future to give input on process improvement, but that time is definitely not now.

- State that you would volunteer to work longer hours or weekends to get up to speed faster, if they thought it would help you in your position.

- Indicate that you look forward to working with experienced personnel in your position and will keep a notebook of suggestions that they offer.

- Volunteer to be included on team projects as soon as your supervisor feels you can bring value, and then state that you will work to make that happen as quickly as possible.

- State that, at this point in your life, you are totally dedicated to making a career, so nothing is more important to you than success. Of course, do not tell that to your fiancé or soul mate, as I do not want to be responsible for those conversations. Believe me!

The All-Important Questions, Bidirectional Interaction

In Attachment 5, I provide a series of questions that you may be asked and questions you should ask in closing the second face-to-face interview positively with the outcome of a job offer in hand. Bidirectional interaction is a fancy term for conversation. In this context, it stresses the importance of relaxing and making the interview as much of a conversation as the interviewer will allow. When the interview becomes bidirectional, a conversation, your personality and enthusiasm can be more easily demonstrated.

Remember, in this second interview, it is all about fit and confidence for both you and the prospective company. The best interviews become conversations, and, by inserting appropriate questions into the conversation, you are gaining a lot of respect from the hiring manager. He or she (or any interviewer for that matter) does not like to do all the work. Who does? If you make his or her job easier by showing interest in answering his or her questions and then asking a question back, he or she is having a discussion across the desk, not just an interview session. Keep in mind that we people are funny animals. We have differing styles, and outside influencers affect our work, so be ready to roll with the punches and give it your all. I have another story for you.

- A friend of mine was in an interview. The interviewer kept looking at her watch. After she did this several times, he politely stated, "I notice you are looking at your watch. Is this a bad time? I would happily reschedule for you." She looked up with a look of relief and apologized, but said she had received an important, but unexpected, call. She stated that she was trying to fit in his interview, as she realized he had stayed overnight in a local hotel and driven three hours to get there the previous day. He told her he would be happy to meet later that day or even stay one more evening, as the job was that important to him. She thanked him and set an appointment for the next day at 8:00 a.m. He got the job, and I think part of the reason, other than that he had followed my advice, was that he noticed her body language was indicating concern over something. He gave her a chance to do what was really important: taking care of her issue first. If he had not been totally attuned, she might have possibly shortened the interview and hurried him out the door with an abbreviated list of questions. He might have lost the job opportunity just because he didn't notice her all-important body signals.

My final advice before you begin practicing your responses to the questions in the attachments is to spend some time thinking about the job and facilitate your own questions, together with my suggestions, both from the company side and you personally. You will have undertaken an excellent preparation if you do this simple task. If you use what you have learned in the first interview and in your research and development, you will find you have a lot more to ask than you think, even as an entry-level candidate.

Closing Your Sale/Getting Checks in the Mail

I won't lecture you on this point, as you have already memorized everything we have covered for closing the sale, right? Before going on, ask yourself, "What do I need to do at this point to close the sale and get that job?" No fair peeking ahead.

You got it! Keep practicing and adding to your pipeline.

Now, assume the second face-to-face interview is over. When the interviewer asks if you have any other ques-

EMPLOYMENT ESSENTIALS College Edition

tions and you have asked the questions I recommend in Attachment 5, then follow through with these actions:

- Thank the interviewer for his or her time once again and ask if there is anything that he or she has asked that needs more clarity, as you would be happy to repeat your answer. Tell the interviewer that you are convinced you can do this job and are willing to take all the steps outlined in your plan, plus, of course, anything the company wants, to ensure your success.

- Reiterate that your background is perfect for this position and that one of the most exciting things you are looking forward to is the opportunity to put your education to work and to learn everything you can about the new position.

- Ask for the job. Plainly say, "I want this position, and it means a lot to me. I am just starting my career, but this job will give me the background and financial rewards to begin a real future with your company." Mention that the company will help fulfill your dream of working in chemistry and fulfill some personal goals. It may sound a bit melodramatic, but, if the interviewer is choosing between two or three candidates, this may push it to your favor. After all, most companies today are looking at growth, and growth is a function of their employees and their employees' stability. If you sound like a mature, advanced-thinking individual, you will be a winner.

At this point, you may be asked to speak with HR, and they will tell you the process to start this all-important first position. They usually require background checks and blood or urine samples for drug testing, so my prudent advice is to pass this last test. Many companies will make you an offer contingent on successful background and drug checks, but, if not, don't worry. Just skip to the next section.

Follow-Up Needed After the Second or Last Interview/Tips to Secure the Job

If they do not offer you the job (and I will be surprised if they don't), your work isn't quite over, but you are getting close. Of course, you will follow up as before, but with some different closing techniques.

1. Send yet another personal thank-you note. E-mail is acceptable.

2. Make a presumptive close by indicating you have taken the liberty to scout out the area, already found acceptable living accommodations, and familiarized yourself with the community and its activities.

3. Ask if people in the company participate in local groups or chapters, like the American Association for Clinical Chemistry and so forth. This demonstrates your desire to learn and participate as a representative of the company.

4. Include everything you have prepared for them in an electronic folder. This is most easily done by creating a zip folder or downloading the appropriate files to a USB flash drive. Attach your résumé, your personal plan, and your references. The references may have been asked for previously but include them in this e-packet as well.

Caution: Make sure you check the files in either the zip folder or stick to ensure you don't send personal files or anything else.

Professional References

References should come from people who know and respect you. Your best friend doesn't hold much weight unless he or she has started his or her own software company and became a twenty-two-year-old billionaire, so leave him or her out. The following references will be sufficient in almost all cases:

- An instructor or two from your college courses

- A prominent businessperson who employed you during the summers or your schooling

- A religious leader, if you are inclined

- Any person of note you may know

Usually, three or four references are fine, and some companies will state the number and type they are looking for. An important point here is to contact and notify these references and give them an overview of what you are trying to do. One of my best references was from a former math professor, and I will never forget it. It helped me get accepted to medical school. I opted for a business career for many reasons, and I am happy with my decision. I now have the experience to share the information in this process with you, and my decision to go into business probably has saved many a life.

Review step 7 of 8
What have you discovered thus far?

---

1. **Review your notes from the first interview.**
   Diligent review and following up with another thank-you
   note stresses your strong points.

2. **Ask for the job in your thank-you note.** Sorry to be
   so repetitious, but those who do not ask seldom receive.

3. **Create your personal plan.** This is a gift for you. Very
   few others will do this, and it shows your ability to perform in a businesslike manner.

4. **Increase the amount of practice and study.** You
   have dedicated too much time and research to slack off
   now. Winners practice more than losers.

5. **Accept the job or prepare for one more interview.**[14] The same as number 4 above, don't quit now. You
   are still in the game.

I think we are finished, and I congratulate you on your dili-
gence to the process, but, more importantly, on assertively
mastering one of the biggest steps in life's journey. I will
be surprised if you do not have an offer in hand, but, if the
decision is made for another candidate, you have just completed what will become the roadmap for success in your

---

14 A third face-to-face interview is highly unlikely for an entry-level
position. In fact, usually one interview suffices, but never stop preparing until you get a written offer letter!

future searches. You have learned the *Employment Essentials* and will succeed before many others because of the work you have done.

Celebrate! You deserve it!

Step 8
Bringing It Back Home/Building Community through the Workforce

This section is optional reading for all, but I feel very strongly about the importance of jobs and the communities in which we live. I recognize you will often have no choice but to move from your community, and that is understandable. I am not suggesting workers stay in a geographic area just because that is where they grew up or went to school, but I am urging young workers to become an integral part of their communities after they join the working world. Our world is changing daily, but one thing that never changes is the vital importance of community interaction. Part of my motivation in writing this guide, as I stated in my introduction, was to create a tool of value for young adults wanting to participate in life through meaningful careers. I believe there is a strong correlation between using a tool like this to gain a career and using that career to benefit others in our communities. Over the years, I have observed that employees involved in their communities, in any number of ways, are usually solid employees and well supported by their companies.

I am currently researching the next directive in a continuing series, which will help guide employees to gain and grow with their companies while benefiting their communities. I hope this work has helped you grow into your career, and I hope you remember the phrase I have used in this document: "You are the product." Your involvement in your communities helps all.

Best of luck in your pursuits! You are a one-of-a-kind product, my friends. If you make yourself shine, your company stronger, and your community proud, it will be a better world for us all.

Attachment 1
Stack-Ranking Your
Employment Search

	Company			
	A	**B**	**C**	**Ranking by Preference**
Location (city)				
Company size (number of employees)				
Field of focus				
Prestige				
Job availability				
Commuting				
Cost of living				
Lifestyle				

I have given this example in chart format, but you can easily create a similar form in a spreadsheet if you want sorting functions, easy addition of other factors, and so forth. I chose the chart format, as I find them fast and easy to use, but it is illustrative only. Refer back to the book to refresh your memory on how to utilize this chart.

At this stage of your life, you and only you can decide what factors are most important to you. My categories are broad by intention, but, for instance, many of you may want to compare job categories so you can research the pay rang-es for the same job within different industries.[15] A start-ing chemist in the pharmaceutical industry may make more than an industrial chemist and so forth. If you are like most job seekers, this will be of interest to you, but I caution against basing everything on starting salary. Unless you have had a lifetime vision of working in a specific industry, go for the job offered, even if it is not in your target industry, to first gain experience. Make that your challenge for today. Other factors, such as relationships and living close to oth-ers, can be separated, but, for me, that falls under lifestyle, and I have it covered. If you use this chart, you will find it helpful for your job hunting and eventual employment.

---

15 As mentioned in the text, you can easily check salary ranges for your job category in the *Occupational Outlook Handbook* published by the U.S. Bureau of Labor Statistics.

Attachment 2
Sample Résumé

You can utilize a simple template, but refer back to my step on résumé building, and make sure your résumé captures the mindshare of the reviewer.[16] I like the following format, as it highlights your education, and, at this point in your life, you have more education than experience.

Date:

NAME

[Type your phone number]

[Type your e-mail address]

[Type your mailing address]

[Type your website]

OBJECTIVES

[Type your objectives]

---

16 For example, Microsoft Word offers simple templates.

EDUCATION

[Type your school name]

[Type the completion date] | [Type the degree]

- [Type list of accomplishments]

EXPERIENCE

[Type your job title] | [Type the start date]–[Type the end date]

[Type the company name] | [Type the company address]

[Type job responsibilities]

SKILLS

- [Type list of skills]

Attachment 3
Sample Cover Letter

Remember, sell and don't tell. You are trying to capture the attention and mind share of the résumé screener. Make it short and simple. You can borrow highlighted points from your résumé, as, after all, you want to catapult yourself above others.

Spectacular Chemistry Company,

I have researched your company, and I am excited by what you offer to your clients. Your work in quantitative chemical analysis, especially in the toxic substance division undertaking the arsenic recovery project, aligns well with my educational background as an analytical chemist with a Bachelor of Science degree in chemistry from State University. My academic work includes the following:

- BS, Chemistry: Graduated with high honors in Top 10 percent of my class

- Achieved the Crystal Beaker award: Recognized for top talent in chemistry

- Awarded laboratory assistant position: Instructed others in lab technique

- Vice president of Chemistry Club: Drove monthly meetings on special topics

I have the following attributes and want to bring them to your attention.

- Self-motivated and highly energetic: Strong work ethic
- Trustworthy and reliable: Concrete personal values
- Excellent problem solver: Challenge myself to find solutions
- Team player: Enjoy working with others and soliciting their opinions

I want the opportunity to demonstrate my worthiness for Spectacular Chemistry. My attitude is both determined and positive, and I am available to speak or meet with you at your request.

Best regards,

[your signature]

Candidate

Attachment 4
Glossary 101 of Business Terms

The following are terms you will encounter in your research and development study and in meetings at your new companies post-hire. This is basic finance, and it is only meant to help you with research. I will only provide an overview of the P&L statements and balance sheet.

Sales and/or revenues: These terms are synonymous and referred to as the top line on income statements.

Costs: The cost incurred is expressed in dollars (local currency) to build a product, often called "cost of goods sold" (COGS).

Expenses: This is the cost of researching and developing (R&D), selling and marketing (S&M), and administrative costs to sell the product.

Profit: This is the amount of sales or revenues left over after the costs and expenses associated with the product or services have been deducted. Profit is referred to as bottom line, and, as indicated below, it should be positive but can be zero or negative. This is not good for the company!

Income statement: This is referred to as profit and loss (P&L) and reflects the amount of profit the company is making/losing on its sales and marketing efforts over a period of time, for example, monthly, quarterly, and yearly. The following example shows that it costs our fictitious company $7,000 on sales of $50,000. That generates a Gross Margin of $43,000. The expenses total $32,500, and they are the summation of R&D, S&M, and administrative, leaving a fine profit of $10,500, or 21 percent of sales. Nice return, graduates!

Revenue	$50,000
COGS	($7,000)[17]
Gross Margin	$43,000
R&D	($5,000)
S&M	($20,000)
Admin	($7,500)
Profit	$10,500[18]

Balance sheet: This is the way accountants measure what companies have (assets) minus what they owe (liabilities) to discover what they are worth (value of company).[19] The balance sheet is really a snapshot of a company's health.

Assets = Liabilities + Worth
or
Assets – Liabilities = Worth

17 Bracketed numbers are negative in that they are costs and expenses; unbracketed numbers are positive.

18 You may sometimes see these numbers represented as a percent of sales. This is called a "common P&L," and it is useful in comparing different companies or past performance within the same company.

19 The balance sheet simply captures a moment in time. That is, it is a dynamic document meant to represent that specific time measured; it changes with each transaction of the company.

It balances because as in any equation, if you add or subtract from one side of the equation, you must adjust the other side to make it equilibrate. The addition/deletion of an asset on the left side of the equation will mean an addition/deletion in liabilities or worth on the right side. This offset thereby balances the equation, hence the name, Balance Sheet.

Without going into detail, the balance sheet is probably the best single tool to measure a company's strength. Many investors look to see how liquid the company's assets are, as liquidity allows them to make purchases or invest opportunistically when needed. For your information, the balance sheet is the only financial statement which reflects a single point in time for a company during their fiscal year.

If interested, many excellent books on financial statements are available online or at the bookstore. One I have found quite useful is *Financial Statements* by Thomas Ittelson. The author clearly explains the meaning behind financial statements in understandable and easy-to-follow verbiage.

If you are really interested in this area, then you will want to invest in a good book on financial ratios, which businesses use to determine strength, stability, investment worthiness, and many other factors pertinent to proper business management. A fantastic book on this topic, *Key Management Ratios* by Ciaran Walsh, is an international best seller.

Attachment 5
Sample Q&A of All
Stages of the Process

I have divided this attachment into sections covering the following:

- The initial phone or screening interview

- The face-to-face interview(s)

- Role-playing tips and model

Initial Phone Screen Commonly Asked Questions:
A Sampling

- How did you find us? Why did you select our company for employment?

- Tell me about your educational experience and how it could relate to the job of interest.

- What courses did you most/least enjoy while in school?

- What do you know about the company and area (city/location) surrounding the company?

- What do you like to do with your free time?

- Are you available to work evenings or weekends if necessary?

- What contribution do you feel you can make to the company over other applicants with similar backgrounds?

- Why should we select you over others for this job?

- What are your weaknesses and strong points we should consider?

- What has been the biggest disappointment you have experienced?

- What is your favorite color, movie, book, or entertainer?

- If you could have dinner with any historical figure, who would you choose?

Blah, blah, blah, blah...blah. You have seen this before, and a large spectrum of questions could be added. The primary lesson I want you to take away is that there are seldom right or wrong answers, but good and bad answers always exist. I will explore this with you. As I so vociferously indicated previously, the first interview results beget the second interview.

For purposes of this interview Q&A, assume the company is Spectacular Chemistry, located in Detroit, Michigan. The company, a chemistry-based testing facility, is primarily focused on quantitative methods for hard-to-determine substances. Their clients range along a broad spectrum of disciplines from clinical to industrial manufacturers. The job description placed on their website required the following:

- Analytical Chemist Position, Spectacular Chemistry, Detroit, Michigan

- Requirements: BS, chemistry or equivalent, with proven quantitative chemistry discipline, augmenting a staff of twelve other chemists focused on analytic detection.

- Skills necessary: A firm knowledge of quantitative chemistry analysis and techniques, including gravimetric and volumetric procedures, familiarity with spectroscopy, mass spec, electro/thermal, as well as the ability to demonstrate strong bench chemistry experiment design.

- Attributes: Self-starter, strong work ethic, team-oriented, good problem solver, creative, cheerful, and honest.

How did you find us, and why did you select our company for employment? I have done my homework. I researched the Detroit area and found your company to be of great interest to me, especially because of the work you do in quantitative chemistry. Plus, your website was extraordinarily user-friendly for finding information about Spectacular Chemistry. Okay, good response, now answer the above question in your words and enhance your response. Then ask again until you feel comfortable with the responses rolling off your tongue. From this point forward, repeat this process after every question.

Tell me about your educational experience and how it could relate to the job of interest. I am happy to share. I recently graduated with high honors with a Bachelor of Science degree in chemistry from State University. As a student, I was selected by the dean of chemistry and offered the paid position of laboratory assistant. I have a great deal of interest in quantitative chemistry, in which your company specializes, and I think, between my abilities demonstrated in school plus my special interest in chemistry in general, I would be an asset to your company. I should mention that I have solid experience utilizing spec/mass spec instrumentation as well as the classical volumetric/gravimetric techniques.

What courses did you most/least enjoy while in school? Obviously, my first love is chemistry, but I also have a passion for math and analysis. These areas were most enjoyable to me. I took a course in art appreciation as an elective, and I must admit I will leave art to others more inclined, so let's count that as least favorite. As a final reminder, now answer the above question in your words. Practice your response. Then ask again until you feel comfortable with the responses rolling off your tongue. I won't repeat this. I promise.

What do you know about the company and area (city/location) surrounding the company? I have studied your website and particularly liked the sections under "Products and Services Offered," as they gave me a good insight to the work you perform. The "About Us" section was thorough and stressed the importance the company places on its workforce. I have lived in the Detroit area, as I attended State University, and like the positive attitude that the area embraces. I am also an outdoor enthusiast, and Michigan offers so much outdoor activity from season to season, a big plus for me.

What do you like to do in your free time? As mentioned, I am an outdoor enthusiast. Biking, hiking, and water sports are my favorite activities, but I am also an avid reader, so it balances itself out.

Are you available to work evenings or weekends if necessary? Yes, of course. I am excited to get started in my career, so I am flexible to the needs of the company.

What contribution do you feel you can make to the company over other applicants with similar backgrounds? Hmm, that is a great question. I believe that, first and foremost, I excelled in my chemistry education. I embraced chemistry, and I have known since high school that I wanted to be a chemist. I spent extra time in the laboratories helping others, and it gave me personal satisfaction to share my skills while improving those of others. I have an intense desire to enhance my education by learning new techniques and the application of those techniques to Spectacular. I am dedicated to unceasing improvement and will work harder than others to attain my goals, both for Spectacular and for me personally. Notice how the question above and following question appear to be the same, but they are not. Can you tell the difference? **Hint:** The first question asks about your contribution to the company; the following asks why the company should select you. In the midst of the interview, you must listen carefully to differentiate so you can give correct responses to both.

Why should we select you over others for this job? I have demonstrated through my education, participation with others, and burning desire to improve that my life's goal is focused on chemistry. I am competitive. I have a strong academic background and want to add value to a company, not just work there.

What strengths and weaknesses do you have that you feel we should consider? For strengths, I am creative in my approach to chemistry problems. I have exceptional skills on the bench, and I am familiar with all classic and instrumental methods of testing. I am not afraid to ask for help if needed, and I have a strong background in analyzing data and then turning it into a useful report. As a weakness, I want to improve upon my knowledge of business, as my plans someday may include management, and I know I must learn more in this area to gain a management role in the future.

What has been the biggest disappointment you have experienced? That is easy for me, as I had my heart set on making the college hockey team. I had played hockey since childhood, but I was cut from the final roster. It was a real blow to me, but I continue to skate for fun and play in local hockey groups. My advice is to refrain from sharing personal information or life's tragedies when answering this type of question. Those types of issues are your business and not the company's. Rather, pull something from your past that is pretty innocuous and let that be the answer.

What is your favorite color, movie, book, or entertainer? My favorite color is orange and always has been. I think I have always favored the color, as it is bright, attracts my attention easily, and fits my upbeat mood. The color is exciting and denotes action. The interviewer only uses this question to see how you think creatively. Answer it with reflection back to a positive trait you wish to demonstrate.

If you could have dinner with any historical figure, who would it be? Without a doubt, it would be Benjamin Franklin. What a unique character, inventor, and statesman. I would love to get his thoughts on the changes in technologies and government that have occurred since his lifetime.

Finally, what are your compensation expectations if we decide to move forward with the next step? I did research using the government information provided on the web that gives salary ranges for specific job categories, but I am not as much interested in the starting salary as I am to start. I am sure Spectacular has ranges depending on experience, so I will defer to company policy.

Okay, that wasn't so hard, was it? The key is that a whole spectrum of questions is usually asked, and you need to be prepared to answer with a relaxed degree of spontaneity without sounding canned. Relax, pause, and then answer.

Don't tire now. You are almost finished, and you will get another interview. You are the best of all candidates because the product is you, and you prepared properly.

Now before we go on, the interviewer will likely ask you one final question:

I thank you for taking the time with me. Do you have any questions you would like to ask about

Spectacular? Yes, actually. Can you describe the process going forward with Spectacular? I really enjoyed the interview with you and look forward to moving on with the company. I want this position, and I want to ask you something. Is there anything I haven't answered fully, as I want to be the candidate of choice? More than likely, the interviewer will say no. You have answered all of his or her questions. He or she will then inform you that they will review your candidacy internally and notify you of their decision.[20] Simply respond, "Ms. Jones, I thank you again, and I am willing to speak at your convenience."

Don't forget what you have learned. Follow up the same day with a written thank-you note, and get it in the mail. Again, e-mail is okay but less personal. Ah, there is love in a handwritten reply. Take a well-deserved break, go to the gym, ride your bike, and have a fast-food binge if you will, but you deserve to get away for a while. Once you're relaxed and your mind is clear, go back and review the suggestions given earlier in Step 6, as your preparation is all important for this next big step.

The Face-to-Face Interview Q&A

Many of the questions could/will be the same as the screener used, but expect to be asked more specifically about what you know and if your knowledge is what the company needs at this point in time. Be ready to be more definitive about:

- The work you have done

---

20 Don't forget my tips in Step 1 if you feel you are being disqualified for the position after speaking.

- The instruments you have used

- Your knowledge of the company and what it does

- How you will benefit the company

- How you will fit to the team

The following will be more directional as to the type of questions a supervisor may ask with detail added. I won't inundate you with responses at this point, as you are already prepared and know what to do. I will give you tips, however, to enhance your preparation. Also, keep in mind that this is written with our test graduate, the chemist with a Bachelor of Science degree. For those of you in other disciplines just extrapolate the question to your field, and it basically comes down to the same questioning.

What? I have to do this again? He looks familiar, doesn't he? One of the most common mistakes, through lack of preparation, is that most candidates prepare for the second interview much the same as the first, a major mistake. Because you know more and are empowered, you will shine in this interview.

How did you find us? And why did you select our company for employment? "I found your company in my research and matched my skills to the job description." Advice: be prepared to further articulate what you have done over and above your answer in the first interview. Use the information I have provided for you. Articulate the steps you have learned; they are priceless, so use them. I won't presuppose your answer, but you have learned so much about job hunting. For the last time, use what you know to enhance your response.

Tell me about your educational experience and how it could relate to the job of interest. Again, build on your first interview answer by inserting more about specific analyses and experiments you did that may relate to the company.

What courses did you most/least enjoy while in school? Be more specific on the courses of interest, for example, discuss why you enjoyed them. Include a brief rundown of the quantitative analysis courses, but mention others you enjoyed, for example, Organic, P-Chem, or Biochem. This is your time to sell, so, the more you articulate, the better. Keep your experience in art as your worst experience as before. Remember to use consistency in answering.

The following questions will be followed by specific answers so that those in all disciplines can easily see the intent of the question and apply it to their fields of expertise.

We do a lot of work in electrophoresis.[21] Can you describe your background in this area? This question determines your depth of subject knowledge.

---

21 Substitute any field. For example, if you are in accounting, the statement might include cost accounting. In marketing, this might be market share analysis and so forth.

Tell me about your lab work, what steps you employ in designing an experiment, and how you would track your progress in a log. This question determines your ability to organize and problem solve.

Oftentimes, our team has to stay late as some incubation times go past normal hours. [22] **How do you feel about a somewhat erratic schedule based on the work we are doing?** This question tests your flexibility and willingness to work.

If you are working under the hood and see that a co-worker next to you is not adhering to company safety policies, how would you handle that situation? This question tests your character traits and workplace problem solving. Caution: this is maybe the toughest question to answer, so get it right. No one likes tattletales, but policy is policy. You do not know your prospective boss's feelings. It is probably best to say that you would politely remind your colleague that the safety policies are meant to keep all safe, and you wouldn't want to see anyone injured because of skipping steps, but also indicate to your prospective boss that you would bring safety up at the next department meeting without mentioning names. If it is flagrant and continues, you owe it to the company and your fellow workers to call the violation out to your supervisor. Most will handle it confidentially, as they are professionals. By the way, your boss should have noticed this also!

---

22 Again, substitute for your discipline. Working overtime in accounting may be for inventory. For marketing, it could be preparing the annual budget and so forth.

We believe strongly in teamwork. Describe your experiences working in a team environment. This question determines whether you are fit for their environment and if you are a leader, follower, or contributor.

Our company is rapidly expanding. How would you feel about relocation to our new site in Fresno upon its completion in the next few years? This question determines your ability to grow with the company. I do not advocate stretching the truth, so the best answer is that you would certainly be willing to consider a move anytime, depending on the job. It is neither affirming nor denying your desire to move to Fresno, or any place else, and you can decide for yourself your willingness to move if such a situation arises.

I am a stickler for detail. Describe the level of detail you provide during a routine process. This question, again, determines if you are process or spontaneously driven.

Many of your co-workers have either MS degrees or are working toward a master's. What plans, if any, do you have to enhance your education in our area of expertise? This question looks for your objectives. Are you focused on your job or career?

What do you know about the company and area (city/location) surrounding the company? The interviewer is using this question to compare your response against your first answer to determine your consistency.

What do you like to do with your free time? Answer as in the first interview. Don't try to impress anyone by saying you like to spend time reading company manuals. It is hard to swallow.

Are you available to work evenings or weekends if necessary? This question determines your flexibility again, just by using a different question.

What contribution do you feel you can make to the company over other applicants with similar backgrounds? This question refers to your first response, so go back, and reinforce your abilities over others. And I do mean reinforce using all the tools that this document has provided you.

Why should we select you over others for this job? This question determines your fit versus all others. Go for it. This is about you. Remember, you are the product. Be sincere and look the interviewer in the eyes while responding. This can make or break you for the job at hand. Use the course work to your advantage. That is, if you tell them succinctly how you defined your goals, tested them for realism, researched the company and area, and developed a personal plan to ensure success, I fully believe that your answer will shine over others. Now put it in your words, and win the job.

If you had to choose to be an animal, which animal would you choose? Truthfully, they are now messing with you, and, unfortunately, many amateur psychologists are in management. If you choose Bengal tiger, you may seem too predatory, and they may want grazers to just blend in. If you choose swan, you may seem too passive, as they may want leadership. But there is no right answer. Perhaps a deer would be a good choice, a beautiful creature that lives freely in nature and runs like the wind. After all, who hates Bambi?

And blah, blah, blah, blah...blah. You are ready for the big day. Feel free to look at volumes of questions available from other sources if you desire, but, as the saying goes, "It isn't the question. It is the response that counts." If you practice the questions I have submitted to you and extrapolate more from your own design, you will knock them out.

Now we go to one of the most interesting challenges prepared for you. Are you ready? This next segment is all important for preparation. With the information you have been given, it will be much easier for you than those who have not received this counsel.

Attachment 6
Mock Interview

Role-playing is like watching yourself on television and being the star.

Role-playing should be fun and relaxed. Choose a friend, teacher, or relative, as indicated previously. Sit at a table and practice answering your questions. It seems a little silly and uncomfortable at first, but it helps immensely.

Throughout my career, I have found that role-playing is one of the most dreaded activities that people have in the workplace. Most are unsure of how to answer questions and do not want to show their weakness to others. Well, guess what? Most people are not natural-born actors, so role-playing takes some focus and concentration and practice, practice, practice. Make it fun!

Give your role-playing partner the questions just reviewed and any others you may want to add or pull from the Internet. There are books of questions available, but you are never guaranteed that the questions you practice will be asked. If you practice role-playing you will be able to field any question smoothly, even if you have not seen the question previously.

Tips for the Role-Playing Partner

You will need to take this seriously. You will help your candidate.

1. Have the applicant walk in and greet you, as in an interview room.

2. Ask the questions in order of receipt (first time only).

3. Now review (with the candidate) his or her answers and ask how he or she felt.

4. Do it again, revising the order in which you ask the questions.

5. Do it again, phrasing the questions differently than the first time.

6. Repeat and practice for about an hour each session, as it mimics reality.

Tips for the Applicant

You, too, take this seriously. It is your job after all.

1. First time through, just answer the questions with the first thing that comes to mind. If you stumble on a question totally, it is okay to say, "Let me start over."

2. Second time through, put everything you have learned into articulating your best answer.

3. Next time, try to answer with more feeling and inflection on the major points.

4. Repeat this process, trying new ways of answering the questions until you find that you can answer the questions without hesitation. This could be several times. Ten or twenty is not unusual.[23]

5. Once you have mastered this process, and if you have the equipment, see if you can record the session and watch your body language. I believe it will amaze you.

---

23 Don't get caught up in a specific number of practice sessions. Practice until you are extremely comfortable. Then break for a day and practice again. No time is better spent in preparing for a job interview.

Attachment 7
Moot Court Interviewing:
Cross-Examining

*H*ow much fun have we had thus far? This is the last
phase of our studies. Bear with me. This is a very
good tool, but few new applicants know of its value.

At one point in my history, I worked for an attorney, and
the lessons I learned have been invaluable to my career. For
example, I learned what I am calling "moot court interviewing," that is, cross-examining yourself, in a sense. While in
law school, the attorney went through moot court sessions,
and it was an honor to be chosen. One thing the students
had to do was to argue both sides of the case equally as well
at separate times. I am borrowing this exercise from that
perspective.

Choose a question from the Q&A that you feel is extremely
important, for example, "What contribution do you feel
you can make to the company over other applicants with
similar backgrounds?"

Now, challenge yourself to critique your answer. Are there
pieces that every applicant could say? The following is similar to my first answer to the question that will undoubtedly
be asked of you: "What contribution do you feel you can

make to the company over other applicants with similar backgrounds?"

I hesitated then said, "Hmm, that is a great question. I believe that, first and foremost, I excelled in my chemistry education. I embraced chemistry and have known that I wanted to be a chemist since high school. I spent extra time in the laboratories helping others, and it gave me a personal satisfaction to share my skills while improving those of others. I have an intense desire to not only rely on my education, but to learn new techniques and the application of those techniques to Spectacular. I am dedicated to constant improvement, and I will work harder than others to attain my goals, both for Spectacular and for myself." Damn, that was good!

Now put yourself in the interviewer's chair and challenge a single piece of your obviously great answer (or so you thought until entering the moot court session, as you are about to see).

Interviewer: "Mr. Graduate, your answer is interesting, but many of our hires have been laboratory assistants and want to learn more. If they did not, we would not be interested in them for Spectacular Chemistry. What is so different about you?"

Okay, now what do you say? It is too far into the process to bolt for the door, and, if you tripped, it would make a bad exit worse. Coming down with the flu this quickly is unlikely, even though you may be exhibiting some of the symptoms. Don't be unnerved. This can and will happen, depending on your answer and the interviewer's style. Many times, the hiring manager is perfectly happy with your first answer, but he or she wants to see what your response will be. Once more, take a deep breath, think about your answer, and then refine or reiterate with even more data.

Mr. Graduate to Mr. Interviewer: "I am sure that many graduates feel that their experience is unique, but I was not the typical lab instructor, nor did I experience the level of concern and caring that I showed to my students from others in this position during my first few years in college. I dedicated myself to the position and felt responsible for the success or failure of those I was aiding. Many times, I set times in the evenings or even on weekends to tutor my peers needing help, and it was totally on my time, not something the university expected. I feel this dedication came from my desire to help and learn simultaneously, and it reflects my desire to excel. Many of my fellow students came to me after the semester and thanked me for caring, as that helped get them through the course. I will carry that same desire and enthusiasm over to Spectacular if given the opportunity."

Nice job, grad!

Okay, I think you get the drift of my message. All answers can and will be challenged. Unfortunately, many interviewers in business get a thrill out of pushing others to their limits just to see just how they respond. Most of the interviewers, however, are just trying to get you to articulate why you are the best, and, if they don't challenge your questions, it may mean they are not that interested or are junior-grade interviewers at best.

This moot court exercise was included so you could cross-examine yourself. Constantly be aware that you can improve on any answer, and try to find the weaknesses in your answers. Then challenge and improve them. If your interview partner is coached beforehand on this section, he or she can and should challenge you while practicing. Be hard on yourself in dissecting your answers. If you are, the real interviews will seem like the easiest part of the process.

Attachment 8
The Never-Even-Think-About-It Topics

You should remember a few rules during the collection of your interviewing experiences.

1. Never speak negatively about any past employment or employer. They may be two-headed monsters, and many are, but there is never a reason to mention it.

2. Refrain from answering any question with a yes or no response unless that is all the question begs. I trained a dog once to tap his paw on the door, indicating he wanted out. For him, it was okay as he gave me a one-tap response, but for you, let's up the articulation, okay?

3. Unless you are pursuing a religious avocation or running for city council, stay away from both religion and politics without question.

4. Realize that bragging in any form is dragging. No one in a hiring position will be impressed, so just keep your ego to yourself.

5. Recognize that you have not bonded with the interviewer. A good interview can be invigorating and make you feel like you have become friends. You haven't. Getting personal and friendly by sharing more than what is required will almost assure your demise.

6. Remember that preparation and a sense of humor goes a long way to success. Prepare, but cut the jokes. You are not doing a comedy routine.

7. Exude passion in almost any situation. If you show it and feel it, it will transcend the interview.

8. Show your stuff, but do not create a situation that requires confrontation at any cost, unless, of course, an interviewer personally assaults you. Sun Tzu, a trusted and respected Chinese general, philosopher, and strategist, stated that most battles may be won without fighting.

Attachment 9
Personal Plan

Personal Business Plan for Jill, Our New Chemistry Hire

> ### Note
>
> I will show three examples of eye-catching, mindshare-developing mini-plans. A simple list would suffice, but you can decide on any of the formats or create your own. For illustration purposes only, I will change the wording slightly to show how you can represent your plan. Remember this: the plan does not have to be a complex, time consuming document worthy of publication. It is primarily a tool to show that you have thought out some necessary steps that you would take to enhance your job performance. In fact, a simple chart or diagram is best, as it is easy to follow and drives your message home. That message, of course, is that you are serious about working for your target company.

Activity Matrix for Full-Time Equivalent (FTE) vs. Time (Plan 1)[24]

Employed FTE	Stage 1	Stage 2	Stage 3	Stage 4
Study company/ department policies	Independent study (off-time reviews)	Saturday: Work in lab to perfect new technology	Co-worker: Learn best practices by asking others in lab	Volunteer: Upon supervisory approval, work for inclusion on project teams to help drive enhanced performance
Month 1: learning phase	Month 1: learning phase			
	Month 2: implement	Month 2: implement		
			Month 3: proficiency phase	Month 3: proficiency phase

---

24 FTE is a term that HR uses to determine head count. An FTE can be expressed as a fraction, for example, 0.5 FTE, indicating an employee working a half-year.

Activity Cycle for FTE vs. Time (Plan 2)

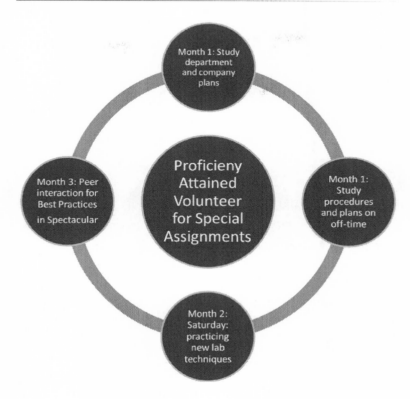

Activity Cycle for FTE vs. Time (Plan 3)

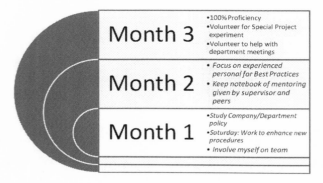

Month 3
- 100% Proficiency
- Volunteer for Special Project experiment
- Volunteer to help with department meetings

Month 2
- *Focus on experienced personal for Best Practices*
- *Keep notebook of mentoring given by supervisor and peers*

Month 1
- Study Company/Department policy
- *Saturday: Work to enhance new procedures*
- *Involve myself on team*

Style is individual. Create your own format in the style that fits your personality. The most important thing is that you show your willingness to attain the level expected by your company in a minimal time frame.

FAQs

Over the course of my research, I was asked some questions so frequently that I have included them again for emphasis. Some questions I did not directly address in the document will be found here.

How long should one wait after submitting a cover letter and résumé to a company before contacting them? It is usually acceptable to give them three to five days to receive your submission. I recommend you call on the third day to inquire about the receipt of your materials.

I am uncomfortable in expressing myself, but I have a lot to offer. What can I do to get more comfortable with the interview situation? Many people are just like you, so relax. The best way to gain mastery of a situation is to over prepare in your interview practice sessions. If you begin to feel comfortable after ten hours of practice, then up it to double that, and you will feel much better. It is also good to change your interview partners so you get comfortable with different people in the same situation.

What should one do if he or she feels sexual or racial tension because of the questions asked or the interviewer's attitude? First of all, today, most companies hold interviews with office doors open as they are blatantly aware of the ramifications of real or contrived charges against them, but it still happens. I advise that you can judge if something was innocently or stupidly said or if the interviewer was indicating more. If it is something that can just roll off your back, bring the question back to the pertinent, and move forward. If you are uncomfortable with the situation, just politely say that you feel uncomfortable and prefer to terminate the interview. Get up, walk out, and send a note to the company's head of HR, recapturing the incident as you saw or felt it. This response will help others, as the company will investigate the interviewer, going back to several interviewees, to see if this issue requires further action. Don't sacrifice your beliefs for any job or company. You will pay down the road if you do.

I have had two interviews for an entry-level job. Upon my follow-up, the company indicated they have been too busy to finalize the decision and will get back to me as soon as they can. Is this a brush-off?[25] They haven't said no yet, so give them some time, but not too much before calling back. As I indicated in the process, go on developing your pipeline of opportunities, but do check in weekly after this point to see if anything has changed with the company. It is also good to resend your credentials and your personal plan to the hiring manager to show your enthusiasm for attaining the position.

I got the confirmation call, but how disappointing. The salary offered is at least 10 to 15 percent lower than what I found in my research for this position.

---

25 Again, refer to my tip in Step 1. Be willing to take a different job in your field at the target company if another candidate fills your job of interest. Persevere by asking.

This makes me really uncomfortable, as I don't know how to handle salary discussions. Help! Okay, let's explore this dilemma. You have an offer, so you must weigh the benefits versus the costs. Are you in the interviewing process with one or two other companies? If so, are you willing to hold out for more money, or do you just want to nail down that first job and deal with the money later? Do you need a minimum salary to relocate to the area? My recommendation is to first decide if 15 percent less is critical to your situation. If it is, speak directly with your supervisor and let him or her know you want the job, but are challenged to make ends meet at the current offer. Suggest something that would fit your range of necessity. If they can swing it and they want you badly, most will come up with the extra money. Typical college grads with four-year degrees earn between $25,000 and $60,000. [26] If your degree begs the $25,000 price, 10 percent is a lot to suffer. If you have a degree that begs the $60,000 range, is it that important in the overall goal of attaining work?

Let's turn the above situation around. You have received two offers, one in an area of the country in which you have never envisioned living, but the offer was substantially higher than the one you received from your dream city. Do you sacrifice lifestyle for money at this stage? Wow, two offers! You followed the program well! This, again, is a personal decision. Remember what I have stated throughout the process. This is your

26 "Bachelor's Degree Salary," last modified July 10, 2011, http://www.payscale.com/research/US/Degree=Bachelor's_Degree.

first job. You can always change once you gain experience. Decision: money versus lifestyle. It's your call.

I am getting discouraged. I have applied to three companies, and I don't seem to get past the screening interview. Do I have a problem? Patience is a virtue. Believe in yourself. If you have followed the aforementioned directives, you will prevail. Never give up! That is the attitudes of winners, and you are much better prepared than your competitors are. You may want to go back to the notes you have taken on those first interviews and look for commonalities in your answers that you could improve. If you have followed my directives, I believe it is just timing and the availability of many candidates for your specific field. Keep the faith. You will find your job soon.

I got the job and have started working at my new company, but in the following week, I got another offer from another company for more money and better hours. What do I do? This is a personal choice. As a leader of companies, I would hope you would align with my company, as we offered first when we recognized your talents. You must decide if the change is worth it to you. Most companies today are focused on what you can do for them, not necessarily what is the best for you. I doubt many companies would automatically match your other offer, as you have only worked there one week, so make up your mind. If you decide to leave, do it quickly and professionally in person. And don't look back. A hint for you: most industries are smaller than you think, and people from separate companies talk and meet at trade shows and conventions, so think hard about jumping after landing a job, as you do not want to be discussed in the industry as a job-hopper.

You have accepted a job, and you are excited to show your stuff, but, upon starting your work, you find you are doing seemingly less-important work than what you did as a laboratory assistant in college. How disappointing, right? There are two issues embedded in this discussion. One is that the company is just evaluating a new employee and will give you more challenging work soon. We all have our personal visions of what our degrees and experience will offer. In truth, most companies start you at positions in which they are assured you will succeed. It's prudent, of course, and wise for the company, as you are just starting, and you must prove yourself as a capable employee. Try to self-actualize, that is, be everything you can be for the job you are in. You will be a great employee, and you will eventually receive more responsibility and the rewards commensurate to the position. The second issue is of a more challenging and serious nature, that is, the company misrepresented to you what the job really entailed. For instance, if you applied for a bench chemistry job in the laboratory and were led to believe that your primary function will be lab work, and then you found that you were spending most of every day in a cubicle calculating the research work done by others, you have an issue.

The most professional way to handle this is to speak directly with your supervisor and just lay it out: you thought you would be doing lab work and wonder when you will get the chance to do that as you seem to be doing mostly clerical work at present. If the supervisor indicates that this is just a temporary duty as they are behind in data assessment, thank him or her and get back to work. If he or she indicates that the lab work has been reduced, and he or she does not know how long this situation might persist, you now have a decision to make. Did he or she know this prior to your hiring or did it happen in the interim between the offer letter and the start date? Either way, you must decide to stay the course, and monitor the situation. If you stay with the company, ask your supervisor if there would be a possibility of rotating the personnel so that you could get some lab experience with the company. It can't hurt, and it is a positive suggestion. If he or she says, "No, it is what it is," then I would seriously start looking for a new position with another company. Business life is ever changing, but if they put you behind a desk and are inflexible in your request to rotate, this is probably not a company for which to plan your career.

Well, at last, you have finished the book, course, or instructional, whichever you prefer. I give you my personal, heartfelt response: If you have taken everything seriously, studied diligently, and continued to fill your pipeline with opportunities, you will not only get a job, but you will become a great employee much faster than others because you have mastered the *Employment Essentials*.

Good luck, my friends! I am with you at info@dadanneassociates.com. My wish is that this work helps you attain your goals faster and more professionally than those not learning the essentials. I certainly enjoyed sharing my experiences with you, and wish you well. Write me to tell me of your successes. I will also periodically answer questions that may pertain to all on my website home page under my blog section. Attachments 1–3 are available to you on my website. Feel free to download them as you create your personal *Employment Essentials* strategy.

About the Author

D. A. Danne is a business executive with passionate feelings toward developing and mentoring people in the workplace of today, inspiring his company's vision of "bringing people, businesses and communities together." He has conducted or witnessed many hundreds of interviews during his career, and he has held several senior executive positions in Tier 1 companies. He currently is the founder and principal of D. A. Danne & Associates, LLC.

13896755R00086

Made in the USA
Lexington, KY
28 February 2012